# BLEAU
# BLOCS

100 OF THE
FINEST BOULDER
PROBLEMS IN THE
FONTAINEBLEAU FOREST

# BLEAU BLOCS

**STÉPHAN DENYS**
TRANSLATED BY NATALIE BERRY

Vertebrate Publishing, Sheffield
www.v-publishing.co.uk

# BLEAU BLOCS

100 OF THE FINEST BOULDER
PROBLEMS IN THE
FONTAINEBLEAU FOREST

## STÉPHAN DENYS

TRANSLATED BY NATALIE BERRY

First published in French in 2020 by Les Éditions du Mont-Blanc
This English edition first published in 2021 by Vertebrate Publishing.

VERTEBRATE PUBLISHING
Omega Court, 352 Cemetery Road, Sheffield S11 8FT, United Kingdom.
www.v-publishing.co.uk

**Front cover** Nico Pelorson attempts *Rainbow Rocket* (8a) at Franchard Sablons.
**Back cover, top left** Florence Pinet on *Septième Ciel* (6c+) at Cuvier Rempart.   **Top right** Baptiste Briand on *La Fissure de la Liberté* (6c) at Gros Sablons.   **Bottom left** Olivier Lebreton scoping out *Le Gardien du Temple* (7c) at Puiselet Sablibum.   **Bottom right** Jérémie Cogan on *Matrix* (7a) at Buthiers Nord.

All photographs by Stéphan Denys (except author portrait by Béatrice Volpert).

Production by Vertebrate Publishing.

Printed and bound in Europe by Latitude Press.

Vertebrate Publishing is committed to printing on paper from sustainable sources.

Maunoury near Larchant, seen from an aeroplane thanks to Jérôme Liabeuf at the controls of a Robin DR400.

# BEAUTIFUL BLEAU

*There are so many beautiful things in this world, but beauty itself is unique.**

What an idea to want to write a book on 'the 100 finest' of Font! Although the principle has been widely used for the mountains, with prestigious collections illustrating the most striking climbs in a region, the Fontainebleau *massif* suffers from such a comparison. It seems incongruous to want to bring together the grandeur of the mountains and their summits with those in the chaotic and minimalist debris of the boulders. Conversely, electing one hundred routes in a mountainous region, however large it may be, hardly seems comparable to choosing from among tens of thousands of boulders and all of their problems. Hence the subtitle of this book referring only to '100 *of the* finest boulder problems' by way of modesty, so presumptuous it would be to define the finest. Apart from these obvious measures of things, even the masculine or feminine gender in the French language determines a difference between these two areas. Between *la montagne and le bloc*, it is so easy to see a kind of opposition, rather than a possible complementarity. If these two geological formations are indeed part of the same world of climbing, they are certainly at extreme ends of the spectrum in the outdoor arena.

In fact, the objective commonality between mountains and boulders is the basic element allowing us to move over them: the mineral. And yet here once again, how can we fail to distinguish between the peculiar sandstone of Font and the granite of most high mountains? On one side a kind of sandpit covered with pebbles, on the other a sort of ice-tray bristling with spikes! Bouldering, especially at Font, is historically associated with mountaineering because climbers excelled at both. Historically, for some, boulders have been a training ground to prepare for bigger climbs, while for others, climbing small rocks is an end in itself. You do not need to see an opposition or a coming-together in these practices, but rather to appreciate their differences. The boulders are easily accessible without any equipment – it's almost natural to want to climb atop small rocks, and so much fun, like child's play. Climbing mountains calls for a deeper, more serious desire, due to the commitment and the equipment required, where the stakes do not have the same consequences. To put an end to all these dubious comparisons, do we not say 'yet, how beautiful the mountains are!' (the lyric is taken from the French song *La Montagne* by Jean Ferrat), but is it credible to adapt this familiar tune to our beloved boulders?

After some forty years of traversing the twists and turns of Font, I certainly do not get the feeling that I have completed the full circuit, as in fully grasping the essence of its beauty. However, I had to try to better define it for this book, by selecting a list of boulder problems. Each climber would quickly concoct their own selection of the hundred finest problems in Font, and it's a safe bet that no list would be identical to another. My perspective is that of an old *Bleausard*, having discovered Font by chance when he was sixteen and immediately fallen under the spell of the mixture of rocks and forest. It took me a number of years to realise the importance of this combination, bringing together mineral and plant. In Font, sandstone mixes with the forest, whether it's logged and worked, or wild and untouched, as it seems to have remained in other places. The great variety of the forest is proof of the impact of this mix on its composition. The ubiquitous vegetation makes the rocky chaos even more inextricable, the forest mesh hides the boulders and often limits the gaze to small expanses, sometimes even causing a feeling of suffocation: a sensation so different to that felt on the mountain and its landscapes as far as the eye can see when you gain altitude. So, a boulder poised at the top of an

* anonymous quote and idiom.

airy ridge, at the end of a gloomy valley or right next to a car park, will not have the same value in my eyes.

As for the route up a boulder – called *le bloc* (the boulder problem) by this linguistic shortcut that evokes a certain fusion of the activity and its medium – I have always felt its beauty to be in its very nature. Of course, there are the different disciplines and styles of climbing, but what hits me most is the fact that the rock offers a path, a 'problem' more or less difficult to solve, always seeking the one of least resistance. In fact, it is very common to find perfectly simple problems, deemed 'pure', at lower grades, because the Fontainebleau sandstone is not stingy with holds and shapes. As the search for difficulty progresses, it is tempting not only to follow the lines of weakness in the rock, but also to find a more or less obvious way up, or one to be defined arbitrarily. Even if there is no lack of examples of 'pure and simple' lines that are high in difficulty, they are inevitably rarer. Bouldering – always looking for the difficulties – is practised in various ways, by sitting at the foot of the boulders, traversing horizontally or even going round in a circle. Bouldering is the scene of all sorts of games, but to me, beauty seems to arise more strongly when the rock presents a single problem on one of its faces.

This vision of bouldering is simply the manifestation of my own perception of an indefinable beauty of bouldering on rock, and it can in no way be considered the best. At least, it aims to put the rock back at the centre of the activity, encouraging people to look at it and better preserve it. It also enables us to give meaning to our climbs simply by considering the rock, rather than needing to follow the direction of a topo. And then, preceding the exceptional character of certain problems, an intimate relationship can be forged with the rock, a story specific to each climber involving nature, rather than so-called 'social' relationships. Visual attraction is therefore important in my perception of the 'beautiful boulder', as a first, very subjective sensation, whereas its objective composition resulting in a unique problem is like a deeper inner beauty. This kind of balance, between the aesthetics of the rock and the beauty of the problem, is becoming increasingly precarious due to people seeking only the difficulty in climbing. The quality of the climbing is also a major part of this search. If, moreover, the climbing itself is exceptional, by its originality, ingenuity or the sensitivity that it requires, then we are touching on a kind of perfection worthy of the greatest routes!

As a child, I dreamed of living in the mountains, and finally these small boulders became real summits. Deciphering their itineraries and wandering through the labyrinths of chaos have become passions in their own right, always with new paths to follow. In truth, this selection of boulders is dependent on my 'vision', even if many other problems could have been added to it. It is above all a picture book, and despite all my work over the last few decades, I am far from having all of Font's finest boulders in my photo library. Similarly, my initial idea was to choose only one boulder per sector, in order to cover the entire *massif* and present the greatest diversity of boulders and climbers, but I couldn't continue in this vein. The simplest ideas can be very complicated to achieve when you really have to put them into practice. Paths less travelled appear, alternative routes impose themselves, some contradictions surface when trying to demonstrate a potential form of beauty. But finally, when it comes to knowing what makes a boulder in Font attractive, the answer is likely unique and specific to each one of us: whatever it is that causes us to marvel at the mere sight of a particular boulder.

**Above** As clear a view as you can get sometimes in Font, Béatrice Volpert on the plateau of La Roche Cornue, in d'Huison-Longueville.

# THE NATIONAL FOREST

# ROCHER CANON

**7a+** **Délivrance**

Right in the north of the National Forest area, Rocher Canon is one of the most popular sites in the forest. Its ease of access and its boulders – generally of moderate height and with very flat landings – have made it a favourite spot for beginners and recreational climbing.

However, it is not easy to choose *the* most beautiful boulder, as they are so numerous and at the same time all quite similar.

This boulder – also known as 'The Matterhorn' – stands out with its sleek slab as though cut with a knife. *Délivrance* is the most difficult line through the centre, but its two arêtes are equally attractive and worth doing.

One of the beautiful beeches of the forest still standing, just in front of the boulder.

Alain Suidi lacking an aesthetic pose, but giving it a go for the photo nonetheless.

# BAS CUVIER

## 6b Erectissima

At Bas Cuvier, the choice of quality boulders is even more complicated. Not that it's lacking in them, this area is full of them – think Rocher Canon to the power of ten – but which ones are really natural? This 'laboratory of movement' as the old guard described it, could also be called 'the DIY workshop', since so many problems have been chipped there. Nevertheless, Bas Cuvier is studded with beautiful faces with perfect landings.

*Erectissima* is an example of the black circuit, on this very characteristic boulder where many problems are remarkable, always demanding the ideal method in order to be climbed. Just to its left, *La Dalle au Trou* of the red circuit describes this face well when seen from a certain angle, even if it is a rather steep and demanding wall for a very vintage 5.

Maël Serre executes the big moves of *Erectissima*.

## BAS CUVIER

**7a** **L'Hélicoptère**

Of all the chipped problems in Bas Cuvier, one of the first known 7s in Font is surely the most climbed. *L'Abattoir* and *Le Carnage* unfortunately live up to their names and were bound to have been natural problems too before being hammered. *L'Hélicoptère* is in fact the natural, direct version of *L'Abattoir* without its chipped holds. A version – or rather a method – found long after the chipping, proving that bouldering, as a practice, can be above all a never-ending search.

Urko Carmona, one-legged, not hesitating to attempt this huge, random and airy movement, with such a nasty fall. The perfect example of making the most of his body on the rock.

# BAS CUVIER

 **La Marie-Rose**

Is this *Marie-Rose* beautiful? She has aged considerably, quite frankly. Yet seeing the number of suitors constantly at her feet, you can't help but notice her success. Is the attraction the historic grade, or simply a genuine interest in overcoming this wall with such sloping holds? It's hard to know. You'll notice the polish on the holds, and then the especially striking, strange cyanobacteria which cover many boulders in Bas Cuvier in a veil of black, the chalk preventing them from covering everything with their dark cloak for a while yet. A necessary evil?

Gérôme Pouvreau, then Florence Pinet, move along the white corridor of the *Marie-Rose*.

## BAS CUVIER

 **7b+** # La Super Prestat

This huge boulder is home to *La Prestat*, the famous 3+ crack striking its imposing north face and one of the monuments of Cuvier in more than one respect. Climbing it from any side is always a sort of adventure, a journey through time and the history of Cuvier, and getting down from it is not easy either.

*La Super Prestat* crosses the big wall just to the right of this famous crack, offering a very contrasting style, all on a slab, consisting of precarious balancing on sometimes-sloping edges. The very prototype of the smooth slab that Cuvier's devotees of yesteryear could surely not have imagined possible.

**Top**  Philippe Le Denmat, a great specialist in the style, at the time of the very first crash pads around 1996.
**Above and right**  Céline Angèle prepares and executes the direct variant of the line, *Haute Prestation*, weighing in at 7c.

## BAS CUVIER OUEST

### 8a Imothep

Slip away from Bas Cuvier by climbing up to its surrounding heights. In its western section, it's often quiet apart from the unpleasant noise of the former Nationale 7 road, and since the 2000s many nooks and crannies have been revisited in order to find new problems.

*Imothep* is an obvious, curvaceous prow that was just waiting to be looked at more closely, with a rather modern climbing style involving compression and heel hooks. A climb that requires strength, of course, but also more tricks, precision and body positioning than it seems, not to mention optimal friction conditions. Add to this good spotting and crash pads, and here is a problem that once seemed perfectly infeasible that today's young mutants will find simply *debonair*, seeking above all to add a sit-start – an ongoing project.

Stéphane Brette (top), Julien Nadiras (bottom), Olivier Lebreton (opposite); each one above an ever-watchful and much-welcome spotting crew for this type of problem.

# CUVIER EST

**5+** **La Digitale**

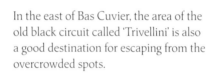

In the east of Bas Cuvier, the area of the old black circuit called 'Trivellini' is also a good destination for escaping from the overcrowded spots.

*La Digitale* is still not too polished, even though it is the archetype of the perfect boulder problem; you basically just have to follow the line! Granted, you gain height and it's a bit scary … Above all, it's best to concentrate on your feet, having eyed the smears, rather than to focus on the crack and the very name of the boulder.

**Left** Olivier Gargominy in 'onsight, I don't want to fall!' mode. **Above** Jacky Godoffe in the 1980s. **Right** Anne Bouchard in successful 'last try' mode.

## CUVIER REMPART

### 6c Duroxmanie

Classic of the classics, and therefore very popular, *Duroxmanie* is a very old 6c whose grade may only increase with the breaking and polishing of the holds. A very pure line where the rock is starting to sculpt naturally more so than the big cubes of the plain, where a poorly chipped and perfectly useless hold can still be found at the top.

Situated at the western end of the great ridge of Rempart, it seems like the opening act. To its left, *La Fissure Wehrlin* at grade 3, then *Le Carré d'As*, a big pillar further to the left, an impressive 6c+ and the finish of the *Trivellini* black circuit, are much less travelled.

**Below** Jérémie Cogan enjoys himself climbing barefoot. **Right** Émilie Moneuse at work and testing her flexibility. **Opposite** Éric Moneuse in the last hard move before the redeeming summit.

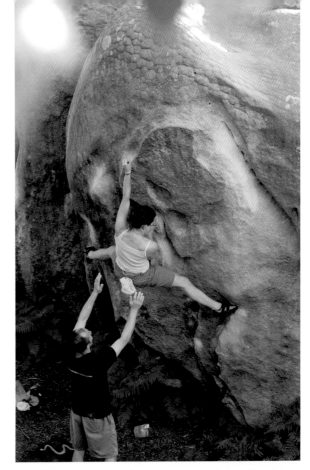

# CUVIER REMPART

**6c+** **Septième Ciel**

Rempart has long offered the highest difficulties in Font, thanks especially to boulders like this one where the very first 8 of the forest was proposed. *Septième Ciel* passes just to the right of the famous *C'Était Demain* in question and even finishes in the same place; the most convenient way to top out on this boulder without getting lost in a gruelling mantel in its large basin at the top. Whereas for the 8a, a high starting position with defined start holds is on the cards, this is not the case for this 'almost 7', whose fairly demanding climbing requires good route-reading and a dose of commitment. This large wall with a slight overhang is almost hidden away in a corner very close to the 'Big Five' and remains less frequented. In fact, *Septième Ciel* is the line of weakness for overcoming this face, particularly well placed despite its height, which is quite rare at Rempart in this moderate difficulty level for the sector.

Nina Caprez and Florence Pinet ascend *Septième Ciel*.

## CUVIER REMPART

**7c** **Fourmis Rouges**

We no longer talk about this spot at Rempart which made the sector famous. And at the same time there would be so much to say about its evolution concerning its beauty, or lack thereof. From the very first – *Big Boss* of the 1980s – to the latest link-ups such as *Super Tanker*, it has a remarkable concentration of about ten problems in the 7 to 8 range spread over four boulders, including the one on the terrace bordering this arena.

*Fourmis Rouges* is one of the oldest lines, on the large airy pillar to the right of *Big Boss*. A fairly perfect line, with complex and varied movements to be executed; an obvious route, and representative of a whole era in which the climbing required a certain level of commitment before the arrival of bouldering mats.

**Top** The 'Big Five' area. **Left** Jacky Godoffe in the early 1990s with his friction-dependent first ascent method. **Opposite** Stéphane Julien demonstrates the 'new-school' version.

## CUVIER REMPART

### 5+ L'Angle Allain

The angle is so perfect that, whether it's with the right or left hand, catching the top always offers a moment of suspense. It also allows you to enjoy the view from the rampart that gave the site its name, located just above, while dreaming of the time when the Nationale 7 road was not so busy, and not the motorway it now resembles.

**Top** A decisive moment for Alex Autexier. **Above** *L'Angle Allain*. **Right** Hélène Janicot tries to trust precarious points of contact.

# CUVIER MERVEILLE

## 8a+ La Merveille

If this big 8a+ is the most difficult route here, all the lines on this boulder are quite marvellous, including even its descent route – fortunately easy given the size of the boulder! *Les Colonnes*, *Le Sourire de David*, *La Fissure de La Merveille*, *La Dalle de Fer* – so many quality routes for this huge boulder that washed up on perfectly flat ground.

The name *La Merveille* was already the name of this entire boulder, and further established itself following the first ascent of its large pillar. A superb line, even if one variant also allows for an escape into the top slab on sharp rugosities.

**Far left** A view of the two largest faces with Lucas Ménégatti giving scale to the height.   **Left** Marc Le Menestrel on the first ascent, around 1999. **Right** Jacky Godoffe at the time of the 'Bloc aux Mille Visages' on *Les Colonnes* (6b).

# ROCHER SAINT-GERMAIN

**7a** **Mise au Poing**

This boulder is known as 'Le Bloc de l'Artificier' (the Munitions Specialist's Boulder) in relation to a characteristic hole which is rumoured to have formed from a shell shot from the plain, but there is reason to doubt the origin of this oddity. Firstly, because it seems so absurd to send a shell flying willy-nilly here, and secondly, because of the concentric deformations of the rock, leading you to think that the rock deformed more like a rather flexible material under the effect of the impact. An enigma perhaps, a certain strangeness in any case making this wall-slab atypical and original. A real school of nubs and precision, crossed by many problems, where it is always best to stay concentrated up until the finish.

Loïc Le Denmat, spotted here by his father Philippe, has done everything on this boulder, to the point of offering 8s with his problem *Lacrima*. In the photo, you could say that he's on *La Dalle du Trou d'Obus* instead of *Mise au Poing*, but what is certain is that he was cruising this slab.

# ROCHER SAINT-GERMAIN

## 8a Vague Patatras

'Vague patatras' (a faint crash-bang) is the noise that often results from attempts at this boulder problem, or even from the descent after success, so difficult it is. It follows a very pure line, to the right of which two more extreme routes have been added. A choice problem on this 'Roche du Barde' (Rock of the Bard) as Claude-François Denecourt named it, and a score that's always tricky for the fingers, also requiring flexibility, precision and even a dose of composure.

**Left and above** Laurent Darlot masters his execution.   **Right** Tony Lamiche will soon make a crash-bang.

# ROCHER CASSEPOT

## 8b Bleu Sacré

*Sacrébleu! Holy crap!* It's not very easy to find such a line at this level in this forest. It wasn't complicated for this one, though, since you only had to follow the blue path to stumble across it. Across this site, many of the boulders marked with a letter by Denecourt are suitable for climbing, such as this 'G' boulder called 'Rocher du Père la Victoire'. *Cent Pofs et Sans Reproche*, a 7c located just to the left, was the first remarkable problem on this face opened by

Didier Gérardin, then Antoine Vandeputte made the first ascent of *Bleu Sacré*. A well-positioned grade 8, which can even be attempted alone. Great Bleausard art on slopey holds requiring the best friction and sequence of movements.

**Left and right** Lucas Ménégatti in full friction. **Below** Guillaume Glairon-Mondet in heel-hook mode.

## ROCHE HERCULE

### 7a Gazoline

At the very gates of the town of Fontainebleau on the north side, just a few steps from the car park, is this aptly named stone colossus. Any visitor, let alone climbers, appreciate it, as the quantity of graffiti and rubbish at its feet regularly testify. The fact remains that this monster boulder is covered with big lines in the 6s and 7s in particular, and even its line of weakness, *Le Gruyère* (4+), or its descent are certainly gifts from the Gods. But why didn't they hide it deep in the heart of the woods?

**Above** *Gazoline*. **Right** Pascal Gagneux, warming up, is already putting his foot on the gas to get to the top of *Gazoline*.

# APREMONT ENVERS

**8b** **La Pierre Philosophale**

The Apremont *massif*, with all its chaos, undeniably offers the greatest concentration of boulders in the entire National Forest as well as in Fontainebleau as a whole. The Âpres Monts, as they were written in the days when the vegetation was not as abundant, offered an image of a desert of piled-up stones. A kingdom of lines of moderate difficulty, the Apremont *massif* nevertheless has some problems of very high difficulty in many sectors. Apremont Envers is in the northernmost part of the m*assif*, an area much less frequented than the classic Gorges.

This Philosopher's Stone offers a strange alchemy … 5+ stand-start, 8b sit! There will be only a few lines with sit-starts in this selection, but this one could serve as an example. If sitting at the foot of a boulder is not 'natural', it is a modern component of the activity that has allowed the level of climbs to rise, sometimes spectacularly, as is the case here. The overhang of this former bivouac was particularly well suited to a sit-start. Whether it is aesthetically pleasing is mainly a question of perspective.

From left to right, Lucien Martinez, Nico Pelorson then Camille Coudert each working the stone in their own way.

## GORGES D'APREMONT

**7b** **Une Idée en l'Air**

This big boulder is also home to sky blue number 1 with which *Une Idée* shares the same start. *L'Esprit du Continent* starts identically but traverses far to the left to escape from this huge face. A very old line completed long before the arrival of crash pads, it's better to fix a rope to work the moves up high, which fits with the name's literal translation of 'an idea in the air', meaning 'just a random thought'. An impressive boulder upon which *La Monte-à-Regret* appeared later, finishing directly up the left pillar, and *Psychose* on the right arête, which is to the left of salmon number 48, *Le Long Fleuve Tranquille*.

**Above** David Evrard during an attempt.    **Right** David Evrard spotting Damien Roguiez getting stuck in to the difficulty for a successful ascent.

## ENVERS D'APREMONT

 **Furtif**

L'Envers is the opposite side of the classic sector of Les Gorges d'Apremont – it is the whole part of the *massif* which faces north – and it's a big area! *Furtif* (stealthy) is what Tony Fouchereau must have been when he decided to tidy up this old and dilapidated bivouac, by clearing out the vast amount of rubbish of all kinds that cluttered it.

It could be called cleaning, while others would call it organisation, it depends. While staying well away from the original construction sites of the Denecourt trails, many recent boulder problems have been created with a minimum of organisation.

The problem can be done by stand-starting off the slope for a very short 7b at the easiest, or from the bottom of the overhang at 8a, with many harder variants.

**Opposite and above**  Tony in compression mode.   **Top left**  A view of David Evrard and the old bivouac table.

## APREMONT PLATIÈRES

### 7a    Le Gong

'How could we let that happen?' This is the question that comes to mind when you discover this boulder and its commemorative plaque. Poised on the heights facing the Platières d'Apremont, *Le Gong* was the first line established by Phil Dumez on this boulder, then came *Véridique* on the left arête of the boulder, then above all *Vive les Femmes* on the right-hand pillar. Many problems nearby are interesting, including the recent *Onde Sensuelle* on a boulder just opposite, which would have been a well-deserved addition to this list. The fact remains that *Le Gong* is one of the 'easiest' on this big boulder, and the meaning of its name should be obvious when trying to catch its key hold.

**Right** Damien Roguiez tries to sound the plaque.

A LA MÉMOIRE
D'UN AMI DE LA FORÊT
GEORGES BOYER
AGRÉGÉ de L'UNIVERSITÉ
MORT POUR LA FRANCE
1889-1916

## FRANCHARD ISATIS

**7b+** # Le Mur des Lamentations

This is the kind of problem that's just perfect! All you have to do is place yourself at the foot of this great face and try to climb it by any route to see for yourself. Right in the centre is the easiest route up this wall. No other rule is necessary, and all the surrounding variants cannot make you forget the purity of this problem.

With a name demonstrating all the inspiration of a certain period, 'The Wailing Wall' suggests both the pain necessary to endure there – its rugosities becoming more and more painful as you progress – and a certain humour when it comes to the more famous wall of a certain religion.

If we had to choose only ten of the most beautiful boulders in Font, this would have to be one of them; even if it really shreds your skin, even if it is too close to the car park, and certainly a little too high to be 'fun'!

**Above** A relatively rare view of this area, as it was deserted at the time. **Right** Nicolas Durand during an attempt.

# FRANCHARD ISATIS

 **L'Arrache Cœur**

7c or harder, given the recent breakage of a hold, this line and very impressive boulder are indeed heart-wrenching, as the name suggests.

The images don't do it much justice and it is a line where the fall is so big that the crash pads often pile up. Yet it was established for a long time before the arrival of these crash pads, respect …

After a fairly easy start consisting of big moves on good holds, a clever kneebar allows you to stretch out towards a crimp over the lip of a roof where the suspense begins.

**Top and above** Mat Sémiond and Tony Lamiche on the key crimp.
**Right** Cédric Chatagnon and the kneebar with the left hand on the hold that has since deteriorated.

## FRANCHARD SABLONS

 **Rainbow Rocket**

Very close to the sector of Franchard Carriers, this boulder has been well-sliced by the blows from sledgehammers and wedges used in the past by the quarrymen. A real school of dynoing, where the whole body takes off from the rock, this face offers increasingly difficult lines the further right you go. The most remarkable thing being its starting ramp, which surprisingly survived the quarrying, and without which climbing on this boulder would surely be impossible.

*Rainbow Rocket* requires synchronisation of a dyno with throwing a foot on to the starting handhold, since the top can't be reached by a simple jump. Dynamic climbing style at its peak, often called 'morpho', implying that it's easier for tall climbers, whereas we couldn't list the moves where it's better to be small and light … Different problems for different climbers, as it goes for all lines. A truly height-dependent climb, so much so that it's impossible to quantify the difficulty for everyone!

Nico Pelorson takes advantage of the last rays of sunshine for some flights.

# FRANCHARD CUISINIÈRE

## 7c+ **Miséricorde**

This is a line that can only make you gasp in relief. Its name, which translates as 'Mercy', speaks for itself. A variant of *Petite Folie*, a line previously established by shifting into the right wall to follow the holds and lines of weakness of the boulder as best as possible, *Miséricorde* follows the line of the very appealing pillar for scarcely more difficult climbing that is ultimately less exposed. It is in fact a more obvious line and an example of the success of a problem often depending on a relative mix of aesthetics and difficulty. This enormous boulder could have given its name to the sector. The holes riddled all over the top of its left face could evoke the big knobs of a giant cooker.

**Above** Wills Young came especially from the Americas to tackle the grattons. **Right** Local climber Antoine Vandeputte devouring this problem like it is fast food.

7a+    **Le Magnifique**

There are some problems whose very name says it all. Even though for a long time it remained 'the unnamed' because its paternity was poorly defined at the time, it couldn't remain without a proper name and a consensus was reached to baptise it *Le Magnifique*.

'Magnifique' is certainly a big word, but this face – seemingly nestled in a box – offers a quality problem. The most striking thing is the variety of styles that its climbing requires: all on crimps at the bottom, and very slopey at the top, with a finish that can even prove to be delicate if underestimated. A fragile and precious problem.

Manon Frébourg and Anne Bouchard alternately try to decipher the problem of this magnificent line.

# FRANCHARD CRÊTE SUD

## 8a Duel

'*Duel* is certainly the most beautiful slab in Font.' A quote extracted from an old video, where, in an emotionally charged voice, its first ascensionist described this line as such.

And as a great specialist of the genre, we can only have complete faith in him. At least as far as the most difficult slabs are concerned, *Duel* wins the prize for the genre, that's for sure. Perfect height, perfect fall, northern exposure to stay cool, a relatively peaceful location, quality holds, a complex sequence and balance; everything contributes to creating an exceptional line and boulder.

But then again, what is more like a slab than another slab? All jokes or mockery aside, if there is a style at Font where evaluating the difficulty by eye is tricky, it's the slab. This *Duel* could just as well have taken place in a 7, or even a 6, as you'd have to be a prophet of rugosities to see the difference without putting your fingers on them.

For the specialists, there are nevertheless all the visible details and differences, but they are simply more subtle to detect than the angle of a big overhang or a pillar.

**Above** Manu Ratouis and his not-any-easier method. **Below** Philippe Le Denmat shortly after the first ascent in pre-bouldering mat times. **Right** The American Paul Robinson in an umpteenth attempt to win this duel.

## FRANCHARD ERMITAGE

**8b+** # La Force du Destin

Among Font's most difficult problems, here is one that could be the very example of a 'pure, natural problem', which is extremely rare at this level of difficulty. Stand start, the line has no possible escape and no easier solution than simply following the holds on this face, leading to a unique problem. Perhaps the start could be even simpler, as it is slightly high to avoid an additional movement, but this is the only minor detail to be pointed out on an otherwise truly perfect line. On its left is *Le Fil de Verre*, graded at 7c+ and also very finger-intensive; this is a quality problem, even if a little too squeezed up against the boulder on its left, the one that must be forgotten about to climb it.

**Top** The problem before it was imagined to be climbable. **Above** Thibault Le Scour (left) at work in the project that Kévin Lopata (right) would end up playing like a Verdi opera. **Opposite** Paul Robinson, one of the few repeat ascensionists.

## PETIT PARADIS

**7c** **Les Thanatonautes**

**Left** Julien Nadiras on his extension of the problem, *Tube* (8a). **Above** Christian Mérimèche builds his feet up before performing the crucial big lock-off of the line.

Franchard's ridges stretch to the east by crossing the D301, becoming the Gorges du Houx. Very close to the forest road known as 'Route des Gorges de Franchard', this boulder is one of the survivors of the quarrying period. This sector – having been favourable for considerable quarrying – contains many bivouacs and remnants from the time when sandstone paving stones were cut from the boulders.

This wall doesn't seem to have been cut, but the boulder on its left indicates that it was narrowly missed! Who knows how many otherwise fantastic, climbable boulders could have been reduced to paving stones? The most difficult problem on the wall, which also offers some good and more accessible problems on its right, *Les Thanatonautes* fell into a slope which has been reshaped thanks to the quarrymen's rejects.

# ROCHER D'AVON

## 7b+ Fil à Plomb

Aurélien Sassier launched into the big move well (above), but missed the good hold on the top;
it is still a big jump before the attempt is successful, in the picture on the right.

The Dame Jeanne d'Avon is definitely the major boulder of the sector, with many exceptional problems. Such is the case with *La Fissure d'Avon*, without any doubt the best 7a of the site, the large, monumental slabs situated on its north face, or the easiest ascent at 2+ of the old orange with a mantle on its strange summit block. *Fil à Plomb* breaches a wall with fierce nubbins to finish with a dynamic movement where each failed attempt brings its share of emotions. Success is very much dependent on bouldering mats and a good spot.

## ROCHER DE BOULIGNY

### 8a+ Gecko

*Gecko* is the most central line of this boulder. Poised like a huge egg and now with multiple variants, there are no less than ten problems on offer. Apart from its two poor arête problems, stand-starting at 6c at the easiest, you won't find anything below 7c, with a number of sit-starts in the 8th grade.

Some will find this boulder ugly, others will find it magnificent, it's a matter of perspective. It is the very archetype of modern bouldering practice, where lines and problems can intersect almost infinitely, as far as the level – and the rock – allows.

**Above** Olivier Lebreton adding the sit-start at 8b+.  **Right** Julien Nadiras establishing the problem.

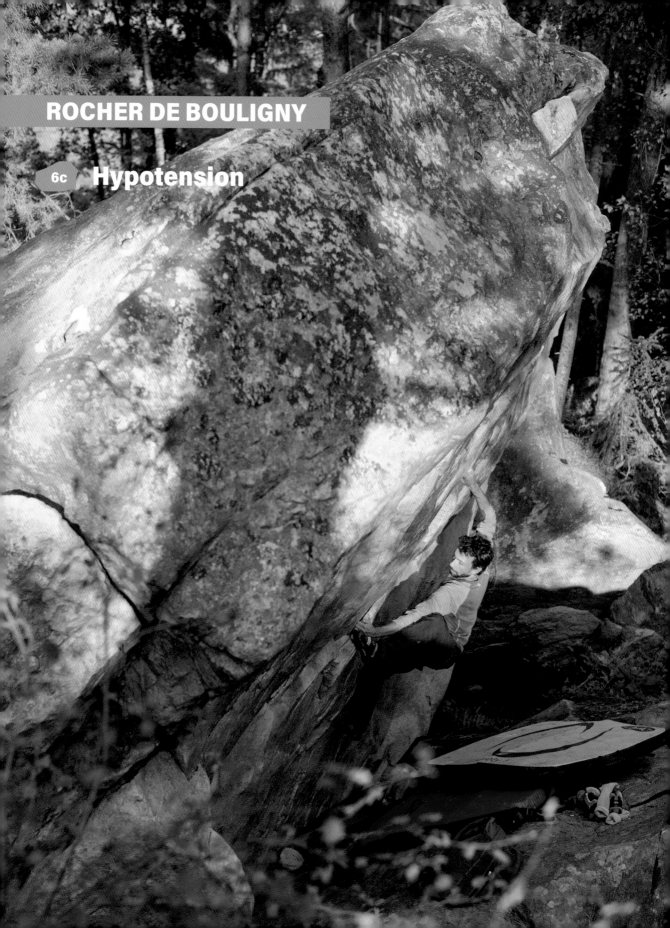

# ROCHER DE BOULIGNY

**6c** **Hypotension**

Directly accessible by following the blue path, this boulder is one of the many remarkable rocks spotted by Claude-François Denecourt when creating his paths. It makes you wonder if 'Le Sylvain' (Denecourt) had the soul of a climber, as many of his listed and named boulders lend themselves perfectly to climbing. 'Les Mazarines', as he christened them, are two boulders on either side of the path, each adorned with a blue star, offering many problems. The boulder of *Hypotension* opened up naturally like a shell, its cut face exposing protruding edges, sometimes causing concern as to their solidity. A small problem that seems to be getting bigger and bigger the more people start right in the hollow of the box formed by the splitting of the rock.

A 'Bouligny Team' in action: Alain Suidi, on the left, then Anne Bouchard, below, under the watchful eye of Pascal Morel who is not at risk of hypertension, enjoying the show from the terrace created by the boulder.

# ROCHER DE BOULIGNY

 **7c** **Les Chevaliers du Chaos**

Lost deep in the central part of the sector, this large boulder, like a monument, is supposed to be forbidden to climb on. It may seem inappropriate to present it here, but as the reason for its ban is to preserve the old 'fresco' that it shelters, we consider that climbing barefoot cannot have the same impact as leaving traces of rubber from shoes. What should we then think about this massive and perfectly banal use of climbing shoes everywhere else?

Is a painted rock worth more than one left in its natural state? A 'fresco' or a 'tag', what is the difference, really? So many questions that can be asked, and to which everyone will answer according to their awareness of the environment and its history. If this boulder really attracts you, let it not be for the ban, nor for the grade, but rather for this swing to be held to climb it, and climb it barefoot like Charles Albert pictured here. By leaving the bare minimum trace of your passage, you will then truly deserve your title of Chevalier de Bleau (Knight of Bleau)!

## 7a  Le Prince d'Orange

These rocks no longer really covet princes and fortunately this boulder is well away from the car park where the dubious meetings of the sector take place. You will have to juggle with an awkward fall and then take responsibility for your desire for isolation until the very end, while guaranteeing success on the last moves, because they are the hardest.

Fabrice Frébourg looking a little bit green as he battles with this very orange rock.

## ROCHER DES DEMOISELLES

 **Le Grand Manitou**

It is not uncommon for the purest and simplest problems to be of moderate difficulty. Font is even a paradise for such climbs. Here, the line is the easiest possible in the middle of this big wall with a slight overhang, offering some big moves between crimps, which it is better to have spotted in advance. It's enough to believe in the Grand Manitou and his genius to have created such a piece of nature to climb, even though it is almost too high!

**Above** Tony Lamiche stretches out right from the very start of the problem.
**Right** Guy Queignec enjoys some fresh air, delighted to have climbed up there too.

# RESTANT DU LONG ROCHER

### 7a  Le Calice

The search for new boulders can resemble a quest for the Grail, the quest for the perfect problem to be discovered. This big boulder lost at the very south of the main sector could have been a real embodiment of it, if only by looking at it from a certain angle to see the famous cup … If only its holds allowed for just a single route, preferably in the very centre of its face, and without any other possible path. Nature decides and it is on these two arêtes that the problems loom, *Le Calice* going up the left one, and *Sol Invictus* (8a) on the right.

**Above** David Evrard started on *Sol Invictus* and then reached the arête of *Le Calice*.
**Right** Frank Scherrer has just passed the crux and is heading towards the good holes at the top.

# ROCHERS DU MAUVAIS PASSAGE

**7b+** **Peter Pan**

**Left** Phil Dumez, who established this quality problem, just before his take-off. **Above** Jérome Chaput holds the swing well so as not to return to Earth too quickly.

All sorts of names are given to problems, and sometimes, as here, they are more or less fantastic heroes or characters from the world of cinema, literature or mythology. Contrary to a name that would describe the boulder itself, these characters sometimes illustrate the type of climbing.

*Peter Pan* evokes the great dynamic movement necessary for this line. There has to be a certain desire to fly, to even believe that it is possible … All climbers are also a bit like children who don't want to grow up and want to remain in an imaginary world.

## MARE AUX CORNEILLES

**8b** **La Cicatrice de l'Ohm**

Arnaud Ceintre in a full endurance effort, first ascensionist of this visibly electrifying traverse.

There will be only a few traverses included in this entire selection, and this one is often considered a 'boulder problem'. However, the problem does indeed traverse, avoiding *Le Petit Et*, a 6b wall on the starting face on the right, then *Acouphène*, a 7a finish skirting the round pillar, before

topping-out by mantling thanks to this line of holds forming like a scarred scratch on this mastodon-shaped boulder. The finish is more or less far to the left according to the first ascensionist who preferred to finish as far along this scar as possible. It's clear the extent to which rules are needed to describe this kind of traverse, even if generally speaking and quite simply; the longer it is the more difficult it is. A major boulder whatever the problem chosen. Unfortunately, given that the area is close to a busy road and therefore has a very quick and easy approach, Mare aux Corneilles is of very sensitive access.

159
ROUTE DE LA
MARE AUX CORNEILLES

# ROCHER DE LA SALAMANDRE

 **7b+** **Menumental**

You have to stand underneath this enormous sandstone slab to wonder how it can still be suspended like this. The climbing here is airy from the first movements and it's a kind of traverse that allows a top-out in the end. A line where you have to keep a cool head and conserve energy until the end, as long as it holds …

**Above** Is it the salamander that gave the name to the site or another monster?
**Right** Frank Scherrer grappling with the beast under very attentive spotting.

## ROCHER DE MILLY

 **7c** # Le Kraken

A fantastic monster, this roof, lost and facing north in the middle of the immense ridge of Rocher de Milly. A sector that could be part of Les Trois Pignons, in fact, if the A6 motorway hadn't drawn its big line of tarmac through the forest. A rare sit-start problem among this selection, as it is especially remarkable for its stratified lower section.

**Above** Gérald Coste in the crux, fully engaging his core.     **Top and right** Manu Marques at rest and then in his committing top-out.

## DREI ZINNEN

 **7c+** # Matière Grise

This problem was nicknamed *Le Mur du Son*, 'The Wall of Sound', before it was climbed, since the noise from the motorway is so loud in this part of the forest! The Drei Zinnen (Three Peaks) are undoubtedly these three big boulders placed side by side. The rock seems to be sculpted like a cerebral cortex, and some *Matière Grise* (Grey Matter) had to be used to pass through the centre of this wall with a slight overhang. The line through the left pillar, *Multipass*, of lesser difficulty (7b) and ending identically, however, came later.

**Above** Olivier Lebreton and the 'three peaks', which likely gave the area its name. **Right** Jacky Godoffe shortly after it was first climbed, around 1998.

# LES BÉORLOTS

### 7c | I comme Irun

**Left** David Evrard in the middle of the crux. **Above** Aurélien Sassier reaches full-span.

This sector is now very sensitive in terms of access as it has been included since 2014 in the extension of an Integral Biological Reserve (IBR). The IBR's objective is to enable the study of ecosystems and the forest environment when they are not subject to human intervention; climbing is prohibited, as is any human activity outside of scientific studies.

The fact is that the boundaries of IBRs are not always well known to the public, especially for those who don't strictly follow the main forest roads, but no one is supposed to ignore them. *I comme Irun* is one of the very attractively shaped boulders of the sector; it was established by Thierry Plaud, a long time before access was prohibited, in homage to his dog Irun who passed away. Should we consider that the boulders in the IBR have had their day, too?

## ROCHER DE LA MARE MARCOU

### 8a Opium

Just on the edge of the National Forest and the IBR of La Vallée Jauberton, this enormous overhanging boulder offers a multitude of extreme problems. All of them are done from a sit-start but are also true problems with stand-starts at their easiest.

*Opium* was the very first problem established and has always been a test of this style of climbing. With its very easy access, it is surely one of the most repeated and attempted passages of this level of difficulty in all of Font.

A drug for all 8th grade contenders.

Iker Arroitajauregi came from his Spanish Basque Country to take his dose of *Opium*, among other boulders.

The Art Of Climbing

OREAL

TROIS PIGNONS
AND THE SURROUNDING AREA

**Rubis sur l'Ongle**

Let's get straight to the point: this line is the prototype of the perfect problem. The problems added long after it was first established don't take away its cachet; neither the one to the left, *Gospel*, because it is much more difficult, nor the easier one on the arête just to the right, called *La Consolation*. All you have to do is stand at the foot and in the middle of this face and want to climb it. The height, landing, positioning and environment all contribute to the quality of the problem. The only downside being that it is far too popular.

**Right and below**  Christian Mérimèche starts up.
**Opposite**  David Rastouil at the crux on the first ascent, around 1991.

# ROCHE AUX OISEAUX

 **6a+** **Le Grand-Duc**

Font sandstone increasingly lends itself to lower-grade problems rather than extreme lines. The physiognomy of the boulders in general, their shapes and wealth of holds, mean that the simplest and most natural problems abound at moderate and intermediate levels.

La Roche aux Oiseaux offers all sizes of boulder, including some of the highest of the Trois Pignons, such as the gully behind *Le Grand-Duc*. An already impressive line, pure and simple, which requires you to commit, but the difficulty is not in the high part if you scope out the finish well in advance.

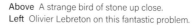

**Above** A strange bird of stone up close.
**Left** Olivier Lebreton on this fantastic problem.

## MONT PIVOT

**7a**  **Belle Gueule**

**Above and top right**   Looking straight at Fabrice Frébourg in the middle of the crux, and the view from his back.
**Bottom right**   Saka the dog leaping for joy while his master, Romuald Bussy, climbs.

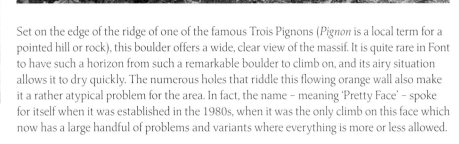

Set on the edge of the ridge of one of the famous Trois Pignons (*Pignon* is a local term for a pointed hill or rock), this boulder offers a wide, clear view of the massif. It is quite rare in Font to have such a horizon from such a remarkable boulder to climb on, and its airy situation allows it to dry quickly. The numerous holes that riddle this flowing orange wall also make it a rather atypical problem for the area. In fact, the name – meaning 'Pretty Face' – spoke for itself when it was established in the 1980s, when it was the only climb on this face which now has a large handful of problems and variants where everything is more or less allowed.

## MONT PIVOT

 **7a** # Le Passeur

Strictly speaking, this is not a major problem but, as is often the case, it depends from which angle you look at it. You have to walk around it to fully appreciate its originality with this curious block placed on its top – a stranded piece of an upper sandstone layer.

The simplest stand-start is reduced to 'fingerboard' type movements for a very short 7a, a start lower down on undercuts bumps the difficulty up to 7c, while the seemingly possible sit-start is expected to be done one day.

In all, a unique boulder offering more lines than it would first appear, and whose history is not quite over yet.

**Above** Pierre Franc on the mandatory big move of the problem.   **Right** Tyler Landman on the more conventional start on undercuts.

## ROCHER DU GUETTEUR

**7a+**  # Le Jeté Pignon

Formerly in the garden of a private property, this rock is so-called Trois Pignons (Three Pointed Rocks) because of its characteristic shape. This property has now been recovered by the National Forestry Office, which tolerates climbing on it. This is a significant boulder which has recently been developed and offers problems of all difficulties. Its large north face offers great soaring flights, but this problem of more moderate height will be more or less dynamic depending on stature and methods.

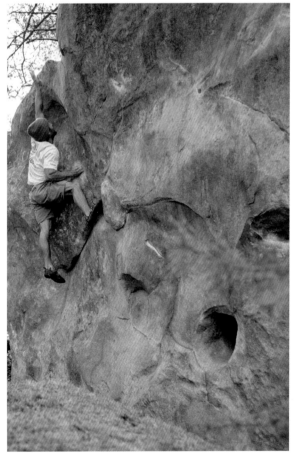

**Top** La Roche des Trois Pignons.  **Above** Julien Nadiras has to find his 'small person' method.  **Right** Tallman Tony Fouchereau executes a big dyno.

## 95.2

**7c** **L'Ange Naïf**

**Left and above** Bruno Guesdon
and Fabrice Frébourg alternately
act as climbing and spotting
guardian angels.
**Right** The strange angel's face
that ogles us with an open mouth.

Offering a big, straight-up dyno, this 'Naive Angel' is a good example of the possible evolution of methods for solving the same problem. Long after it was established around 1984 by Alain Ghersen, a more static and easier method with a heel hook was found, then once again a simple hand switch on its key crimp made for an ever easier sequence. It would be very naive to believe that the search for difficulty is easy! Any line, no matter how pure it seems, can be optimised thanks to new methods, and this is what makes for the most interesting aspect of outdoor bouldering for some people. For other climbers, it's all about trying different problems, as if repeating what has been proposed is all that matters. These climbers will then be able to try this dyno from the angel as it was first done, with both feet down low in its mouth.

# GROS SABLONS

 **Bibop**

Bebop is indeed a very difficult style of jazz music. You have to follow a wild tempo, be able to play complex and often improvised phrases, regularly changing harmonies, and therefore have great technical mastery.

This vast overhanging wall of Gros Sablons left little room for improvisation, the only other problem being about five metres further to the right, the particularly exposed black number 23 called *Le Suppositoire* (6b).

Highly adept at dynamic and rhythmic climbing and gifted at two-finger pockets, Stéphane Brette found this line to his liking. Some twenty years later, a sit-start was added.

**Above** Stéphane Brette on the first ascent. **Left** Olivier Lebreton establishing the sit-start at 8b. The photographs are about twenty years apart; the birch tree on the earlier photo is no longer with us.

# GROS SABLONS

**6c** **La Fissure de la Liberté**

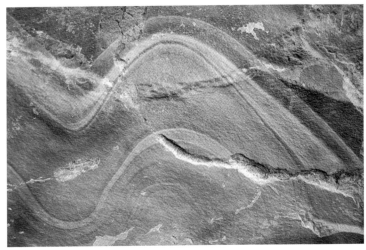

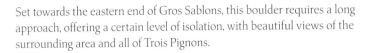

Set towards the eastern end of Gros Sablons, this boulder requires a long approach, offering a certain level of isolation, with beautiful views of the surrounding area and all of Trois Pignons.

A large handful of lines pass through it, but its crack is what stands out at first glance; the very obvious line of this 'Crack of Freedom', once simply called *La Liberté*. A track to follow, whatever the method, a perfect example of a 'pure line'.

**Above and top left** Baptiste Briand and Fred Nicole follow the line.

## ROCHER DU POTALA

**8a** **Le Surplomb de la Mée**

The boulders keep changing and are often more fragile than they appear. This overhang has suffered several broken holds, while ultimately remaining climbable thanks to new methods.

If *La Fissure à Puck*, 5- and blue number 47, is its easiest route, all the possible lines to its left are in the 8s with a distinct tendency to get harder and harder as you move away from this line of weakness.

A serious and impressive boulder depending on the conditions, it is a milestone for very high difficulty at Font across the eras.

**Above right** The direct method of Marc Le Menestrel.
**Top and above left** The current method with Julien Nadiras and Olivier Lebreton.
**Opposite** Iker Arroitajauregi during a late session.

## CUL DE CHIEN

**7a**  # Le Toit du Cul de Chien

**Above**  David Evrard takes advantage of the summer to revise his classics.    **Top right**  A view of the *bilboquet* from the top of the roof.
**Bottom right**  The 'star problem' of an era on the cover of a 1989 magazine and a 1999 video.

This roof – so close to the emblematic sandstone *bilboquet* that gave its name to the site – isn't showcased in the media any more. It's undoubtedly one of the most picturesque and most-visited places in Font. A problem that was 'tweaked' for climbing a very long time ago (around 1978), and it can't be said whether or not it was possible to climb it in its natural state. Many times it's been daubed with paint, graffitied, chipped and then filled-in again, then re-chipped, and it's always very busy – all costs of its success and popularity. A unique boulder in itself with various other striking problems, this one in the centre of the roof is like a rite of passage to the 7th grade. Crossing this roof never leaves anyone indifferent, neither the climber nor the often numerous spectators at their feet.

## CUL DE CHIEN

**7c**  **Éclipse**

For a forest with few real roofs, the Cul de Chien is an exception with these two remarkable problems in this style. *L'Autre Toit*, 'The Other Roof', as it was called before its very first problem *Arabesque* was established, is now full of problems and link-ups, like a section of an indoor training board in the open air. *Éclipse* was one of the first lines climbed without tinkering with the rock, even if a rock on the ground was later buried to make the fall more practicable, and the starts ultimately clearer. There's a choice of either a stand-start at the easiest, or beginning as far down as possible to increase the difficulty into the 8s. You may wonder how this big cigar of a boulder can hold such an unstable position? Looking at it from the side we can see a big ball that seems to counterbalance it on its back base and we have to hope that this assembly will last.

**Top left** Fred Nicole at the birth of the starts from the back of the roof. Julien Nadiras (top right) and Christophe Laumone (above right) in the final dyno. **Opposite** Paul Robinson on the ceiling.

## J.A. MARTIN

**7b+** **L'Étrave**

If a boulder were to illustrate the concept of a 'pure problem', the pillar of this one would be a perfect example, at least at this level of difficulty.

As the practice of bouldering becomes more and more complex, with many problems becoming more defined and contrived, this bow embodies simplicity itself. Standing on the ground and attempting to climb it is the problem itself. Regardless of the method, here the rock dictates passage. The line is obvious, and perhaps the climb takes on its full meaning here.

**Top** Patrick Edlinger, probably the first ascensionist of the line.   **Above** Olivier Gargominy provides scale and focuses ahead of another try.
**Right** Sylvain Péchoux during his very first success.

## ROCHER CAILLEAU

### 7c Alien

On this large overhang, perfectly placed on flat ground, many problems arise, including this sit-start. Straight ahead on the left, *Vandale*, an already difficult stand-start at the easiest, which becomes even more complicated when sitting at 7c. *Vandale* is in fact the finish of this *Alien*, which starts on the right side of the boulder, or else becomes a little easier by topping out immediately on the right …
If you're not following this, don't worry, it's all very 'alien'!
This boulder is full of problems and ultimately the most difficult one is the one in the middle at the highest point, the *Cœur d'Alien*, which is already a low 8 at stand-start and can go up to 8b according to the variants in sit-starts. This is a good example of boulders that always provide a choice: for the climber who is looking for the grades to decipher a topo, for the one who is attracted by the rock itself and wants to climb through it any which way they can, or all the intermediate practice variations.

Climbing on a large *macaron* that landed from space; Pierre Franc, above, and Vincent Pochon, on the right.

## ROCHER CAILLEAU

### 6a+ Le Vit d'Ange

Of course angels have no member! It's just there for the bad play on words, a practice so dear to some Bleausards, and a name obviously inspired by the very characteristic shape of this boulder standing there proudly in a remote corner of the area.

There are several eliminate routes through it, but, to make a long story short, the simplest is the best. Start standing, then move straight up on big, fragile holds; the difficulty will seem inversely proportional to the size at first sight.

**Above right** The remains of old aid practices.   **Opposite** Timothé Denys on the big holds that shouldn't be pulled on too hard.

 **8c**

# The Big Island

Between *The Island* that Dave Graham had opened and the one that Vincent Pochon made big, it's just a matter of start positions. The first one pushed on the boulders behind the problem, the second travelled the island simply by starting with feet on the ground. The next and final step was the sit-start, done by Simon Lorenzi for an even greater isolation, with what he called *Soudain Seul*, proposing the 9a grade! The fact remains that without these boulders forming a terrace under this overhang, working the moves, brushing, or examining the holds would be quite different,

and the problem might still be in gestation. Without these set-back boulders, the problem would also be of absolute purity, even if at this level of difficulty it doesn't look too bad – the stand-start from the terrace being the only easy alternative as a warm-up. A line that requires you to just ignore these set-back boulders to become perfect. On its left side, the problem *Sérénité* at 7a+ doesn't disappoint, just like a few metres to its right, the amazing *Conviction* (8a) is also to be attempted from the true floor.

**Top** Even Dave Graham felt a little stretched on his island.  **Below** Lucas Ménégatti during his 'big' success.
**Right** Pascal Gagneux shortly after finishing with this big bugbear.

## LONG VAUX

 **Fata Morgana**

On the north side of this great ridge, many boulders are worth making a detour for. This one, although old and still hard, was one of the first to become a reference. Except for a 7a on the far left, everything is very difficult on this boulder, and you really have to conjure up fairies or devils to hold on to it.

**Left** Christophe Laumone, first ascensionist and discoverer of this *Fata Morgana*.　　**Above** Antoine Vandeputte loses core strength but still succeeds.

## ROCHE FEUILLETÉE

### 7a+ Superheavy

What a strange name for this beautiful orange face that's so well situated. La Roche Feuilletée is in fact the southern part of the crest of Long Vaux. The rocks here are like *mille-feuilles*, especially at its eastern end, where they have not been cut by the quarrymen exploiting the sandstone. Who knows the number of boulders that could have amazed us but were cut into paving stones? Placed at the farthest west end of the sector, with a decent height and beautiful view of the plain of Milly, this remarkable wall is an isolated survivor of the quarrying. Its climbing is not as tough nor as 'heavy' as it seems the more you stick to the right side, but its location is really 'great'.

**Above** the clearing in front of the boulder.  **Top and right** Catherine Miquel discovering the problem.

## VALLÉE DE BOISSY

### 7a+ Les Nombrilistes

South of Les Trois Pignons, this valley leads to the small village of Boissy-aux-Cailles. Bordered by wooded ridges hiding numerous sandstone outcrops, it is a preserved area where climbing must remain discreet and respectful, always being aware of moving on potentially private property. As is the case almost everywhere outside of the National Forest, the woods are often hunting reserves, and boulder hunters do not have priority there. At the place known as 'Château Renard', you have to go down to the very end of a valley to discover this large, smooth and finely sculpted slab with this strange hole as though in its belly. The original problem allows you to escape to the left; the direct is a test for the fingers and requires considerable commitment.

**Above** Frank Scherrer during attempts at the direct 7c line before the last movement, the worst.   **Right** The 'navel' is visible under his feet.
**Top** Discovering the boulder.

126

## BOISSY-AUX-CAILLES

### 8a+  Hip Hop

**Above**  Iker Arroitajauregi, a regular Basque Spanish visitor, tries the sit-start, while his dog Lhür has lost faith.
**Right**  Olivier Lebreton at the time of its first ascent at the very end of the last century.

The Butte de l'Église was the very first climbing spot in Boissy, partly due to its easy access. Situated towards its summit, it is a shock to discover this boulder the very first time, especially when you don't expect it; this large rock offering so many possibilities at a high level. This mound holds many other problems as well of all difficulties, but this is the only one where mosses never grow back too quickly.

*Hip Hop* is one of those 'pure' problems, and it took a 'new school' style of climbing to solve it. A perfect natural route, a stand-start without constraints, an obvious sit-start, no exposure allowing you to even work the problem alone, with a moderate but far from ridiculous height. A line that could embody the more dynamic style of climbing that new generations have brought to Font.

## VALLÉE ALLAIN

**6c+** **Grand Large**

**Above and top right** Bart van Raaij, the 'Flying Dutchman' of Font, gets to grips with the crimps on *Grand Large*.
**Bottom right** Boissy's 'cailles' – pebble inlays in the sandstone.

Close to the village of Boissy-aux-Cailles and far in the depths of its Allain Valley there is no shortage of boulders. Thierry Guéguen, a tireless pioneer, has done the most work in these sectors where the mosses always return faster than the climbers for the farthest boulders.

This wall of *Grand Large* remains frequented thanks to its exceptional character, even if the problem is rather painful on small and thin crimps. Fortunately, several problems allow a gradual warm-up on this face.

## MARLANVAL

### 8b Éléphunk

Sit-starts are rare in this selection. A lower extension of the 7b problem called *Mach 4*, sit-starting where holds permit from the ground then offering a sequence with a good degree of higher difficulty. It is characteristic of sit-starts to increase the difficulty of all 'normal' problems, and this practice which seemed so incongruous in the past has become widespread on all boulders. Sometimes, as is the case here with *Éléphunk*, this kind of start is comfortable and quite obvious as the holds of the problem are facing the ground, while sometimes they make for contrived additions or add little of interest. A mini area nestling at the bottom of a valley bordering the village of Marlanval, on the borders of the Seine et Marne and the Essonne and Loiret rivers, this spot has very few boulders but this one won't let anyone down when it comes to its great aspect.

**Below**  Chris Schulte when the whole valley had undergone a major trimming of its vegetation.
**Right**  A few years later with more greenery and Pascal Gagneux during an attempt.

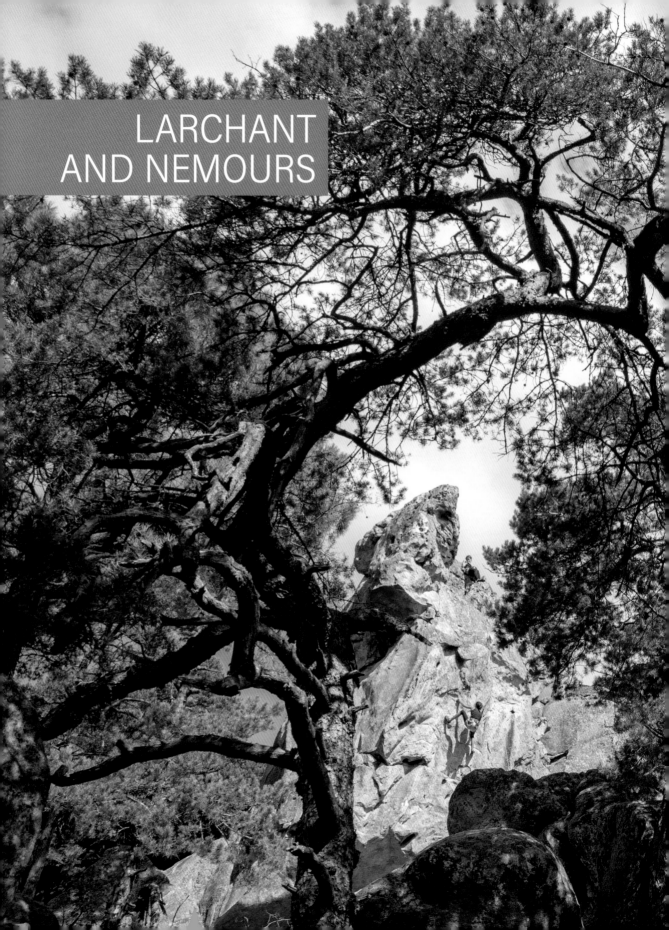

LARCHANT
AND NEMOURS

# DAME JOUANNE

**7b+** **La Tour de Babel**

The 'gulf' of Larchant is known for housing the largest boulders of the Fontainebleau *massif*. Just like a large cirque formed by a vast depression leading to the marshy plains, the rocks here are heavily sculpted, as though manipulated by a now invisible ocean.

François-Xavier Joubert and Gérald Coste take on the tower.

Just below the Dame Jouanne boulder, which is currently forbidden to climb on as the erosion has become so concerning, stands this 'Tower of Babel', stranded on the slope. An unrelenting problem all about wide spans and toe- and heel-hooking.

## DAME JOUANNE

**7b** ## L'Angle Parfait

With a name like that – 'The Perfect Angle' – there's nothing to add nor take away! A very old line, which is among the most remarkable of the site and is always a technical and somewhat mental challenge. Only *L'Angle Plus que Parfait* is able to cast a shadow on it, as it is situated directly opposite and even more perfect, so they say.

**Left** At the end of the gully, Pierre Raynal makes another attempt.
**Right** Antoine Chevalier struggles against the barn-dooring.

# MAUNOURY

**7c** **Irréversible**

**Left** Julien Nadiras at the time of
the line's origin around 2002.
**Above** Stéphane Brette, who first
unlocked the key sequence,
during his successful attempt.

In keeping with Dame Jouanne, Maunoury also harbours boulders of considerable size. *Irréversible* required some adjustments, as the many boulders at its feet made the fall impossible and the problem rather offputting from the outset.

Teamwork is as important as climbing on such problems, where crash pads and a good group of spotters make all the difference between launching up for a certain point of no return or jumping off while there is still time.

# MAUNOURY

**7a** **Waimea**

It is not uncommon for boulderers to feel a kinship with surfers. Like surfers, boulderers are highly dependent on weather conditions, and their activity is based around an entirely natural element. As in surfing, a 'tribal' spirit can inspire boulderers, so much so that helping each other and building strong, collaborative relationships enables climbers to progress smoothly.

The sandstone formations in Larchant are so tortured in places that you could imagine them as petrified waves. However, we are far from Hawaii and the surf spot that the name of this problem evokes. This sandstone breaker doesn't move, but sliding on it is quite possible, as is being thrown out of the roller! Once on its upper part, everything is calmer.

Franck Fortuné and Thierry Bouchard alternate attempts to catch the wave of the problem.

# ÉLÉPHANT

**7a+** **Arcane**

Of all the rather incredible shapes that boulders can take, there are some particularly bestial ones, such as the all-too-famous Elephant of this area, which is also now forbidden to climb on like the Dame Jouanne due to erosion problems. In fact, the entirety of the great cirque of Larchant is undergoing heavy and rapid erosion, but this is always more visible in its increasingly frequented sectors.

*Arcane* is one of those problems that can seem delicate, with the crux unfolding on rather thin holds, and like everywhere else it is better to avoid throwing yourself at it anytime and anyhow. Otherwise, *La Diagonale*, which passes just under this kind of archway is an alternative at the same level with a very different style.

In turn, Loïc Gaidioz and Tony Lamiche discover the mysteries of the Elephant.

# ÉLÉPHANT

## 8a Partenaire Particulier

Jacky Godoffe bounding at the end of the 1990s, crash pads having replaced the backpack; on the right the big key lock-off of the passage. On the huge block on the right, the left arête is *Le Pilier Légendaire* and the middle of the face is *Haut de Gamme*, 6c and 7a+ respectively and equally superb.

The Éléphant sector overflows with imposing boulders and this great wall was for a long time a 'seemingly impossible' project, to paraphrase a cult quote from its first ascensionist. From the start the problem was, as it were, starting, and Jacky Godoffe made the first ascent by jumping off his rucksack on the ground, creating what was a stiff 8a for the era.

Much later, Christian Roumégoux found a solution to start cleanly from the ground and add this + to the difficulty, but the fact is that the sand keeps escaping in this sector, making the start of this problem really odd. The fact remains that this big face catches the eye and overcoming it is exclusive to just one problem, whatever the method chosen at the beginning.

# ÉLÉPHANT

## 7a Le Cœur

'All shapes can be found in Nature.' A common expression that can be proven at will, but which always comes to mind when the rock evokes more familiar forms of the animal world.

The diversity of the sandstone's formations gives rise to occasionally disturbing configurations, where we can see monsters or equally morphological representations. Is it a game of chance or a hidden message? Go figure.

Here there is no need for hallucination, as there's not just a hint of resemblance to the well-known, simplified form of this essential organ. The rock seems to wear its heart on its sleeve.

It is striking to note that on such a pure line, this hold is also an essential one, and that you could cover every bit of rock without ever being able to come across such a perfect shape again. Unique.

**Left and above** Alex Autexier takes care of this big heart to get a better grip.　**Right** Stéphanie Bodet during an attempt.

## ÉLÉPHANT OUEST

 **5+** **La Dalle à Poly**

**Right** Philippe Ribière struggling with this giant Gruyère cheese.
**Below** A 'stolen' snap of an unknown climber.

Anything but a slab, this Gruyère! And what a 5+.

The fact is that by climbing up by the easiest method and to the highest point, no hold is bad and the difficulty lies in not rushing it, always keeping a bit in reserve.

An exceptional hunk of rock unique to the southern part of Font.

## BOIS D'HYVER

### 6c+ Lame Fatale

**Above left** Théotime Guesdon walks on the silica crimps. **Above right** François Louvel repeats this problem that he discovered a long time ago.

There is always a great originality and diversity of styles in the areas within the gulf of Larchant. The sandstone and its sedimentation are more fragile than in the north of the Font *massif*, and this is certainly what makes the rocks here often very 'sculpted'.

The line of this *Lame Fatale*, 'Lethal Blade', takes place on large silica flakes which led to the dislocation of the boulder to form this imposing roof. Lost in this area of Bois d'Hyver, well away from more frequented areas, this boulder is also covered with problems of lesser difficulty and this line is especially valuable for being the most direct and fairly committing.

# LES ROCHES DU PARADIS

**7b+** ## Les Veaux Ressuscités

Thierry Plaud and Laurent Darlot
'resurrecting' this problem.

The road from Larchant to Nemours runs along a huge sandstone ridge to the north, which is not very well travelled. At Le Puiselet, there are vast sectors which are often neglected, both due to the generally very impressive character of the boulders, and also the fact that they are essentially north-facing, with one of the wildest atmospheres where mosses and lichens quickly grow back. Is this really paradise?

This group, formerly known as the 'Séracs' and the 'Radius', regularly falls into abandon, but still offers a few major projects. This large boulder with its characteristic basin is in the centre of the sector, enthroned on its terrace, and was among the first lines opened by the Allayaud brothers during the establishment and rediscovery of the sector.

## MONT SARRASIN

### 7a Biotope

The first historical spot in the Puiselet sectors, Mont Sarrasin forms a large gable covered with often-immense boulders, which has given it the reputation – rightly so – of being one of the most exposed climbing areas of Font.

However, some major boulders of 'human' dimensions can be found there, such as this *Biotope*, nestling among other imposing boulders on the north side of the gable. A problem with an off-centre dyno where it is better not to be too small, of course, and demonstrate good dynamic skills. A surprisingly pure and natural line.

**Top** Ruins on the eastern access road to the sector. **Above** Pascal Morel demonstrates the problem. **Right** Phil Dumez at full stretch.

## PUISELET SABLIBUM

 **Le Gardien du Temple**

On the eastern part of the village of Puiselet the ridge extends to a point where the boulders begin to resemble small cliffs. This wall of La Sablibum is so big that it could compete with the biggest boulders of Font. It is mainly equipped with pitons and anchors that allowed for training on a rope before a closer look was taken at this demanding and natural line worthy of a 'Guardian of the Temple'. The problem avoids the direct finish, which would transform this climb into a solo, traversing instead to the left until the mantel on its characteristic ledge, the difficulty being in reaching this ledge.

Olivier Lebreton scoping out the line, and then on the first ascent of the problem.

## PUISELET SABLIBUM

### 8a Démonia

'Always higher, always stronger.' A doctrine pushed to its peak with so-called 'highball' problems. Lines made possible by systematic rope work, numerous crash pads and just as many good friends to spot.

*Démonia* is a high point of this style and of an era, even if since then yet more direct variants have been added.

Julien Nadiras on the ladder for cleaning and inspecting the holds, then on a very first attempt.

# PETIT BOIS

 **6c** **Big Jim**

Le Petit Bois de St Pierre is one of these more recent areas that were immediately a big hit.
The speed of access to the site, its coolness when the temperatures rise, and the quality of
its boulders and circuits explain its success.

This imposing wall of *Big Jim* can be seen upon making your first steps into the area.
And, despite its moderate grade, it requires precise climbing, especially as the difficulty
builds to a crescendo, ending with some huge moves.

Lisa Rands (left) and Ben Sémiond (above and right), two visitors to Font and *Big Jim*.

## PETIT BOIS

 **La Baleine**

This 'Little Wood' is home to many large sandstone mastodons. The name of this one, 'The Whale', suggests that it is a giant ocean creature, and it is certainly all the more so considering the difficulty of climbing on to its back.

An often-slippery whale with a crux on small, round crimps that are difficult to grasp at first sight.

Tiphaine Boussaingault (top) on the very physical start, then Tomasz Kozaczewski (above) and Guillaume Giraud (right) both facing the trickiest moment of the problem.

## ROCHER GRÉAU

 **Les Conquistadores**

Standing in the Parc de Nemours like a sort of ogive, this boulder catches the eye initially due to its sharp arête called *Mégalithe* (7c), located just to the right of the wall known as *Les Conquistadores*. Two problems of the same quality but with quite different styles, each of which requires a certain level of commitment. An emblematic boulder of Gréau and this region of Nemours, whatever the attraction of the line or the difficulty sought. Further to the left is a problem at 6a called *Cocotte Minute*, 'Pressure Cooker', which allows you to test the inevitable rise in pressure on this kind of large boulder.

**Above** Alain Suidi negotiating the crux section.
**Right** Anne Bouchard during her conquest.

## VALLÉE CASSE-POT

### 6c La Roche Tremblante

**Left** David Evrard at the steepest part of the overhang for a stiff 6c that packs a punch.
**Right** François Louvel takes another approach for the same difficulty.

The Bois de Nemours, a vast estate containing a number of remarkable boulders, is already the 'deep south' for Font. The sandstone formations are increasingly crooked, sometimes fragile, and often with original shapes such as this species of mushroom balanced on its pedestal. Who knows how long it will remain like this without tipping over? The aptly named *Roche Tremblante*, 'Trembling Rock', can be climbed on all its faces, with problems ranging from 5 to 7 depending on the variant, without a problem really being named. It's a Bleau adventure without any information, to sum it up.

# VALLÉE CASSE-POT

## 6c+ L'Étrave Casse-Pot

A high arête lost in the middle of the valley that borders the south of a large sand crater, this bow *(étrave)* offers physical and airy climbing. The 6c+ betrays how the difficulty varies between 6c and 7a depending on your size and – or – form of the moment. This is also the finish of an original traverse incorporating three boulders that has been established to create *Trilogia* (7c).

**Above** Olivier Lebreton at the point where it is best to escape to the right of the boulder.   **Right** Fabien Marchand appears serene in suspension mode.

# LES MAMMOUTHS

**7b** **Osiris**

There is not really a pyramid in these areas and even less gods or mythical kings, yet this boulder installed at the end of the ridge is certainly one of the most revered of the sector. The connection with Egypt is the 'Egyptian' movement that can help with the deep lock-off to reach its small crimp, in profile, like a hieroglyphic character. A boulder offering on its opposite side the famous and just as pure problem – *Ubik* – tipping into the pantheon of the 8th degree.

**Left** A local pyramid very close to the boulder. **Above** Stéphane Julien in the Egyptian method.

# FOSSE AUX LOUPS

### 6c Le Bouffon

There is a good chance that everything will have to be rebrushed in this sector of La Fosse aux Loups. Access is difficult because it is remote and, in this Forest of Nanteau, you have to be willing to get lost in order to find your way around.

Moreover, the chosen name of the problem here, 'The Buffoon', is unlikely to be motivating. Yet the boulders of this valley are worth the visit, and this face is not a joke, offering in addition *La Fissure Enchantée* (7a), just on the left, which *Le Bouffon* joins at the finish.

A line of weakness in this rock, this is the purest problem, seemingly more difficult than it really is, which doesn't spoil anything, quite the contrary. Its right-hand variation, *Super Bouffon*, is no more super in substance than the extra difficulty it offers, around 7b.

Pascal Morel makes a face to play the buffoon.

## ORMESSON

 **7c** **Stupido**

Exploration is the basis of all discovery and to close the chapter on this great region of Larchant and Nemours, what better than a hitherto unknown boulder? This large boulder offers multiple problems, from 6 to 7+ and, at the time of writing, a few projects. *Stupido* sticks to the left aréte and its fall will certainly have inspired its name.

Manu Marques at work on a direct version of *Stupido* on a bitterly cold day.

# BUTHIERS
# AND ESSONNE

## BUTHIERS NORD

### 7a Matrix

A summer session for Jérémie Cogan.

Buthiers is a grouping of a good handful of areas including this northern part, which is one of the most recently developed. The conditions are pleasant in very hot weather, but its location just above the road leading to Malesherbes unfortunately makes it a noisy spot.

The sandstone is fragile here and lacks silica, and the boulders are often very sculpted and have a round and welcoming shape. The climbing is therefore quite physical, with big overhangs and roofs with often low, deep-set starts, depending on whether you want to enter a certain 'matrix' or not.

## BUTHIERS PISCINE

### 8a Atomic Playboy

Traverses can be self-evident, or indeed eliminate, depending on whether the rock actually guides you along a sideways path, as problems don't always lead straight up vertically to the top.

This long plateau rim situated far to the west of the classic sites of Buthiers is a very old example of a striking line in this style, with its ramp of holds to follow, suspended like a petrified sandstone wave. A Fontainebleau roller wave upon which you can imagine that you're a playboy surfer for a brief moment.

Christophe Laumone and Catherine Miquel, a couple in life and on the boulders, are great *connoisseurs* of the forest, pictured here in the last century.

## BUTHIERS PISCINE

**7b  Master Edge**

With its leisure area including accommodation, camping, a planetarium, swimming pool, climbing wall, and so on, the Buthiers *massif* sometimes takes on the appearance of a circus. You wonder what this wide valley looked like, everywhere lined with huge boulders, at a time when no infrastructure occupied its plain.

In this part near the swimming pool there is a considerable number of remarkable problems, *Master Edge* being one of the most 'accessible' examples of the 'La Duchesse' group. All around this very pure pillar, each and every problem is a symbolic masterpiece of the area.

**Left** Pierre Raynal commits above good spotting.   **Above** Kajsa Rosen succeeds on the dynamic crux.

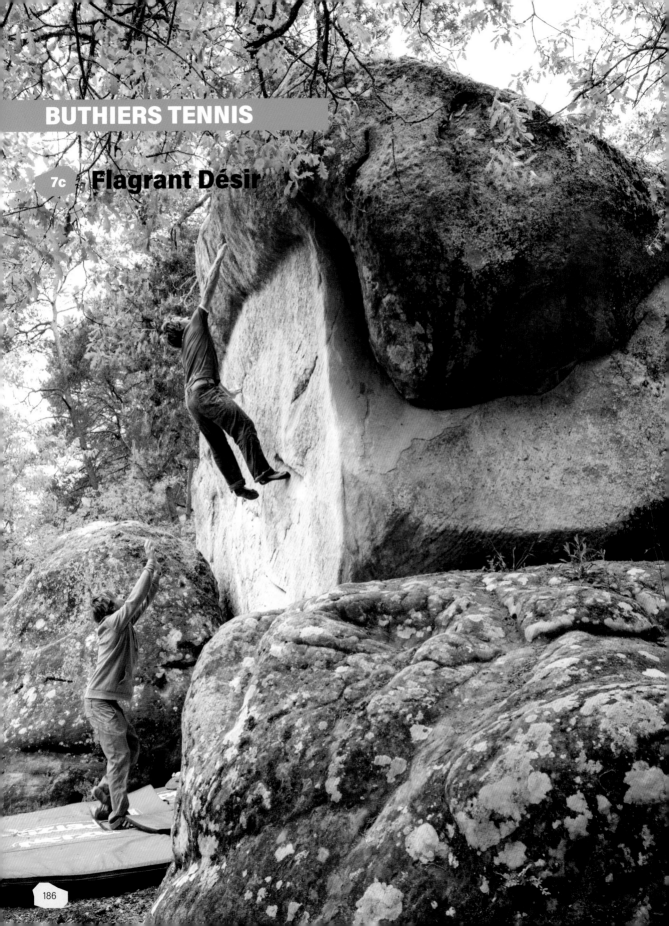

**7c** **Flagrant Désir**

Right next to the tennis courts is this large boulder, with one white side as though bleached by the sun. An old line from the 1980s opened by Alain Ghersen, at a time when everything was yet to be done on all the boulders. Just on the right is a much more recent problem, *La Ligne Blanche*, less difficult at 7b, but more exposed.

Loïc Gaidioz gets going with a huge move in his *Flagrant Désir*.

## 7a  Attention Chef-d'Œuvre

What more can I say? This problem is indeed a masterpiece and the photos do not do it justice. 'Attention' perhaps also because of its height, and above all the purity of the line is notable, right in the middle of a wall, surrounded by the arêtes of *Partage* and *Persévérance*, 8a+ and 7c+. Finally, it is also fortunately a little bit away from the leisure area, even if its access is very easy along the small road leading up to the village of Auxy. A masterpiece first climbed by Jean-Pierre Bouvier a long time ago.

**Left** Damien Roguiez at full extension.   **Above** Christophe Bichet uses other techniques.

# CHANTAMBRE

**7a+** **Démembrure**

David Evrard, 'boulder hunter', rediscovering this *Bloc du Transformateur* and its *Démembrure* passage opened by Eric Letot.

It takes a certain willingness to explore to get away from the great areas that are known as the most famous, classic sites, and the whole Essonne Valley offers a lot of sectors that are not recorded. Many spots here are secret, to preserve their wild side, which means that their access is not always well defined.

On the northern slope of the small hamlet of Chantambre there are a few isolated boulders, the most striking of which is shown here. *Démembrure* is one of the lines on this large piece of rock, which also offers more than a good handful of other more accessible problems that are just as remarkable.

## TRAMEROLLES

 **Anakin**

Olivier Lebreton on *Anakin*, the easiest version of this boulder, which can be quite scary and can be extended by climbing across from the right arête to become *Skywalker* at 7c+/8a.

To the south of Maisse and its climbing area Le Patouillat – a well-known sector with plenty of boulders – is the Tramerolles Valley. It's an even bigger spot, but one where private land, and above all, hunting grounds, do not currently allow for a broad disclosure of its climbing. Small red arrows mark many problems, traces of the pioneers of the sector,

and the quantity of exceptional boulders could make it one of the major areas in Essonne. But just talking about it here could be a source of problems, so it will always be advisable to be as discreet as possible, to climb with the least possible impact, and that the force be with those who show an utmost respect for the place and all its users.

## BOIS DE MALABRI

 **Sol Carrelus**

All around Maisse, sandstone rocks and ridges have been exploited for more than just climbing. Where the boulders have not been cut into cobblestones, the quarrymen dig up all the sand in the deepest part of the subsoil. Nevertheless, there are still many notable small areas and boulders in this large Bois de Malabri. Here too, access is sensitive but you can get lost and still find a number of quality boulders.

View of the quarry on the Plateau de Maisse (top), very close to this cut boulder, where Aurélien Sassier focuses on his foot placement (above), before jumping like Damien Roguiez (opposite).

## BOIS DE MILLY

 **Haute Pierre**

**Left** Haute Pierre's east and then west side with its iron ladder.
**Above** Thierry Vasseur and his unique method of climbing this
*Haute Pierre*, much to the amusement of his companions
who established the sector in the 2000s.

Very close to Milly-la-Forêt but well hidden in the heart of the woods to its west is the landmark rock known as 'Haute Pierre' (High Stone). Its name reflects its position – it used to be a natural lookout offering a great view of the vast plain of Milly, which the vegetation now partly conceals. Its overhanging east face offers some rather athletic lines and an airy finish. The boulder itself is worth the long approach for its many problems of all levels.

## VIDELLES LES ROCHES

**7b+** **Olniak**

The Essonne is not just about secret or modestly sized sectors – as shown by this great ridge of Videlles les Roches, which can easily be compared to the most important *massifs* of Font. The chaos and boulders of Videlles are impressive; this element of wildness to the place – with few car parks and facilities – is what makes it such a well-preserved area. *Olniak* is right in the chaotic centre of the village sector and it can either be started very directly or by the red problem situated just to its right for a notch lower in difficulty, while the end of the climb requires a tricky sleight of hand.

**Above** The chaos and atmosphere of Videlles, where much remains to be discovered.
**Right** François Louvel and Hélias Millérioux, great trailblazers of off-the-beaten-track climbing areas.

## PUY SAUVAGE

**7b+** # L'Arête Secrète

**Above** The boulder in the middle of the hunting area and its surrounding environment over the seasons.
**Right** Fabrice Frébourg in the middle of the crux.

'Secret' spots – aside from deliberate desire for personal ownership – are often 'secret' because it is not always clear whether they lie on private or public land. It is tricky to know whether climbing is tolerated there, making word of mouth the best way to disclose them.

These sites do not lend themselves to mass practice; discretion, respect for other users – often hunters – and for the places, must be the main concerns of those who practise in them. This must always be reiterated, even for those who seek a certain level of isolation and the most respectful and 'natural' means of climbing as possible.

*L'Arête Secrète* is one of the monuments of these wild lands. It would surely be better not to show any here, but how can we ignore some examples of exceptional boulders isolated far away from the National Forest boundaries of Fontainebleau, especially when these boulders are no longer really secret due to the internet?

## BOIS DE BAULNES

 **Chasse Gardée**

The desire to 'do a boulder' or to succeed on a line should always hinge on the authentic emotion it arouses in each climber. Difficulty, an element of the activity, sometimes takes precedence over the boulder itself and what it really offers.

Very close to *L'Arête Secrète*, this impressive problem and boulder were opened long after this initial secret. The season is very short, outside of hunting periods, for finding the boulder in good conditions, and it requires plenty of motivation to get into it.

Aurélien Sassier was waiting for the end of the hunting season to try and succeed on the problem.

## 7a+ Forêt Noire

There are so many boulders that could be included from this vast domain of the Grands Avaux Forest and its Rochers du Duc (The Duke's Rocks). These woods are home to numerous sites, so intertwined that even their names have become mixed up.

The name of this problem – meaning 'Black Forest' – is apt! Far removed from the great, overcrowded classic sectors of the *massif*, this slab is isolated on the north face of the ridge behind the famous Chaumière du Télégraphe restaurant.

If there were a 'top 10' list of Font slabs, this would have to be one of them. Its central line is a typical example of a 'pure' problem, its colours contrasting well with its serious location and uncompromising difficulty.

Timothé Denys giving it a go, discovering the mini round and sloping holds in this 'Black Forest'.

## MOULIN DE ROISNEAU

### 7b+ Twin Peaks

It takes one last traverse to complete this list of problems that rank among 'the most beautiful of Bleau'. This boulder is however too high, too big, too monstrous and it is very difficult to choose one line over another, as so many impressive ones are on offer. Set on the heights just above the Essonne river, it offers a great view of this valley.

Olivier Lebreton begins the airy climb towards the finish after a long rising traverse.

# EPILOGUE

At the end of this selection and this book, it is high time for me to do some accounting. First of all, with the grades and this number of 100 problems. I never thought it would seem so big. One hundred seems very few compared to the number of boulders that Font tallies, but it quickly became a huge number when it really came down to choosing a final selection. Then there are the grades for the problems presented in this book. It may seem elitist not to have chosen to include more accessible problems. Counting the grades of these 100 climbs shows that this selection gives pride of place to the number 7, surrounded by some 6s and 8s in equal parts, with very few 5s and nothing below. I hadn't thought of making these calculations before I had finished my mission, and I have to admit that problems at easy grades are absent. This is a fact and it will seem to somewhat contradict what I said in the Introduction, about my interest in natural and simple lines, which could not be better represented than at the lower levels of climbing difficulty. A primary reason for this form of elitism is that I would be quite incapable of having to choose among the multitude of easy climbs at Font. How can you choose from the thousands of lines of low difficulty? Most of them are very pure, so should I have chosen them just for their appearance? What's the point and what's the angle? For their history? Aren't there already a few books on this subject? It seems to me that all circuits and their authors already do this better than anyone else. For any beginner and even very experienced climbers, if they don't feel any particular attraction to this or that rock, all they have to do is follow arrows. And then, in all honesty, I also realised that I had very few images depicting these so-called easy boulders! Either I don't really like these images and they are not worthy of a book, or they are only suitable for preserving personal memories.

In fact, this lack of representation of less difficult problems, after these few figures, also leads me to consider my words

… I wouldn't know what to say about easy climbs, except that I find them very beautiful! They are the problems that invite us to climb when we discover bouldering by ourselves. A crack draws its line and leads us; an arrangement of footholds and big jugs leads us up a stone path, and here we are already at the top of a boulder. There are countless examples of perfect problems that require no words to define them at Font! A large part of the popularity of this place is surely due to the fact that the sandstone lends itself well to accessible lines which nonetheless require some learning. This is such an important aspect of climbing, having to look for methods, to find sequences of movements to adapt to the rock, and not the other way round. But now I have to talk about images, since this is the main purpose of this book, because it is by our gaze that we judge all beauty initially. To accurately represent aesthetic problems in photographs has never seemed easy to me, and even less so for easy boulders! It is very surprising to see regularly how deceptive photography can be. Faced with a problem that you judge to be aesthetic you will often be disappointed by the resulting pictures; whereas an insignificant, even ugly problem can be quite enhanced by a skilful shot. Boulder photography is a rather disconcerting and often disappointing practice. I have been aware since my beginnings in this field that it is difficult to make progress, in all senses of the word. But what progress, or rather, what major technological transformations have appeared over the last few decades! If I've had the chance to see these transformations up close, it's fundamentally because of Font, but above all because of all those who have helped me over the years. This epilogue is above all an opportunity for me to thank all those who appear in this book. As well as the many people who are not in it but who have helped me just as much, from my very beginnings in Font until now, in the hope that they will recognise themselves. To all of you: thanks! That's all.

In alphabetical order, climbing on these pages are:

Charles Albert (68, 69); Céline Angèle (10, 11); Iker Arroitajauregi (88, 89, 109, 128); Alex Autexier (22, 148); Christophe Bichet (189); Stéphanie Bodet (149); Anne Bouchard (15, 51, 67, 167); Thierry Bouchard (143); Tiphaine Boussaingault (164); Stéphane Brette (12, 105, 141); Baptiste Briand (back cover, 107); Romuald Bussy (97); Nina Caprez (18); Urko Carmona (6, 7); Arnaud Ceintre (78, 79); Jérome Chaput (77); Cédric Chatagnon (45); Antoine Chevalier (139); Jérémie Cogan (back cover, 16, 180, 181); Gérald Coste (82, 137); Camille Coudert (35); Laurent Darlot (28, 57); Timothé Denys (119, 204, 205); Phil Dumez (76, 157); Nicolas Durand (43); Matthieu Dutray (56); Patrick Edlinger (114); David Evrard (36, 38, 74, 86, 110, 168, 190, 191); Franck Fortuné (142); Tony Fouchereau (38, 39, 101); Pierre Franc (98, 116); Fabrice Frébourg (71, 96, 103, 201); Manon Frébourg (50, 51); Sébastien Frigault (54); Pascal Gagneux (33, 121, 133); Loïc Gaidioz (144, 186, 187); Olivier Gargominy (14, 114); Guillaume Giraud (165); Guillaume Glairon-Mondet (30); Jacky Godoffe (15, 20, 25, 85, 146, 147); Dave Graham (120); Bruno Guesdon (102, 103); Théotime Guesdon (152); Hélène Janicot (23); François-Xavier Joubert (136); Stéphane Julien (21, 173); Tomasz Kozaczewski (164); Tony Lamiche (29, 44, 72, 145); Tyler Landman (99); Christophe Laumone (112, 122, 182); Olivier Lebreton (back cover, 13, 64, 84, 94, 104, 108, 129, 158, 159, 170, 192, 193, 207); Loïc Le Denmat (27); Philippe Le Denmat (10, 52); Marc Le Menestrel (25, 108); Thibault Le Scour (58); Kévin Lopata (58); François Louvel (153, 169, 199); Fabien Marchand (171); Manu Marques (82, 83, 176, 177); Lucien Martinez (34); Lucas Ménégatti (24, 30, 31, 120); Christian Mérimèche (61, 92); Cathy Miquel (124, 125, 183); Émilie Moneuse (16); Éric Moneuse (17); Jo Montchaussé (111); Pascal Morel (156, 174, 175); Julien Nadiras (12, 60, 65, 100, 108, 112, 140, 160, 161); Fred Nicole (55, 106, 112); Sylvain Péchoux (115); Nico Pelorson (cover, 34, 46, 47); Florence Pinet (back cover, 9, 19); Thierry Plaud (154, 155); Vincent Pochon (117); Gérôme Pouvreau (8); Guy Queignec (73); Lisa Rands (162); David Rastouil (93, 111); Manu Ratouis (52); Pierre Raynal (138, 184); Philippe Ribière (151); Paul Robinson (53, 59, 113); Damien Roguiez (37, 40, 41, 188, 195); Kajsa Rosen (185); Aurélien Sassier (62, 63, 87, 194, 202, 203); Frank Scherrer (75, 81, 126, 127); Chris Schulte (132); Ben Sémiond (162, 163); Mat Sémiond (44); Maël Serre (4, 5); Alain Suidi (3, 66, 166); Antoine Vandeputte (49, 123); Bart van Raaij (130, 131); Thierry Vasseur (197); Béatrice Volpert (xi); Justin Wood (209); Wills Young (48).

**Top** 'Climber or rock, which one observes the other?' Justin Wood spotting Franchard Cuisinière's *Karma*.

# MAP

In the table above, * indicates a sit-start and † a traverse.

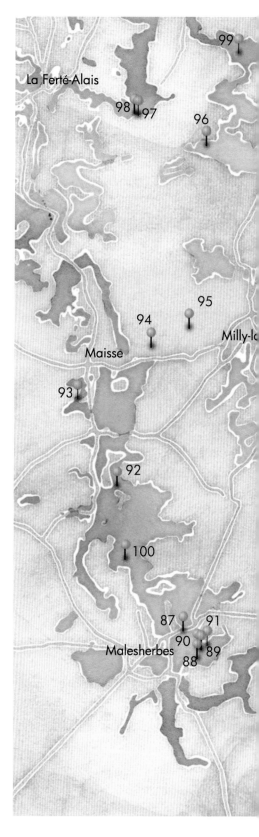

Fontainebleau
- Avon

Larchant

Nemours